T0304367

SHARE THE WEALTH

SHARE THE WEALTH

Maureen Thorson

velizbooks.com

Veliz Books' titles are available to the trade through our website and also our primary distributor, Small Press Distribution (800) 869-7553. For personal orders, catalogs, or other information, write to info@velizbooks.com

For further information write Veliz Books:
P.O. Box 961273, El Paso, TX 79996, USA
velizbooks.com

ISBN: 978-1-949776-10-2

Cover image: *Pyrus communis* © Royal Charles Steadman (1923) U.S. Department of Agriculture Pomological Watercolor Collection. Rare and Special Collections, National Agricultural Library, Beltsville, MD 20705

Cover design by Maureen Thorson and Silvana Ayala

Printed in the U.S.A.

CONTENTS

✧

✧

☼

No one can win all
the time. We advise
you to play merely for
pleasure and to risk
only what you can
spare.

—The Management

✧

If your time to die has come
and you die—very well!
If your time to die has come
and you don't—
all the better!

—Sengai Gibon

SELF-PORTRAIT AS PEASANT

All the women in the bookstore's café
wear chunky hand-knit cowl scarves.
Mine is turquoise and silver, bright as a pool full of dimes.

Us bookshop ladies wear our Saturday hair
loosely piled and held with clips,
crowns of black and blond
and brown and gray.
Leafing through novels, clutching coffees-to-go,
we are the little empresses of our own attentions.

From a display of new arrivals,
I catch Martin Luther's round brown eye staring at me.
I can tell he's thinking I'm a pool
that isn't very deep.

But can he tell I'm thinking about the scene in *Andrei Rublev*
when the Golden Horde attacks?
A cow on fire runs through the middle of town,
past peasants full of arrows
who just a moment before were browsing paperbacks, enjoying
        their coffee . . .

Not that Rublev ever painted peasants. He only painted God.
For peasants, you need the elder Bruegel.
In his painting *The Peasant Wedding*, no one really knows
who the groom is—

it could be the man in a dark jacket in profile, in the center of the
        scene.
Or the pop-eyed youth slurping soup to the bride's right.
That's how unimportant the groom is—he disappears.

I've lived a life that disappears.
I drink coffee, I read, I chat.
Daylight lays its scarlet camellia in my panties.

Night slides its lily fangs against my throat.
I am watching history

but I'm no Luther, no Rublev,
not even Bruegel painting a scene.
I'm a dancer, a drinker, an unidentified groom
wondering if that red fleck outside the window
is supposed to be sunrise
or a pitch-dripping arrow,
the first cow gone up in flame.

MPH

A torn and badly-folded map, memory
shows us places we've been
but not
      how we got there
certainly not where we're headed

under the tremulous sky of
Aberdeen or America
the beautiful as I suppose
or maybe just the map's label for what's not really there, like
      Narnia or England—

but still I'm
all in for the journey,
blazing. Anterior and apposite as a smooch.
My way is the highway
and lacks a speed limit.
      When the exit signs swim past
catching your rearview in the green glow
of a radioactive swamp monster or hope
"Whither the snows of yesteryear"
"You better have a good explanation for this"

      Where asters
      burst in purple fireworks
      and lilacs snort like horses

There's decent eating on this landscape.
India ink shadows in the orchard

apples that practically glow
like gas fireplaces, red
and blue and artificial.
I'm like, well. Okay.
Maybe your ship's come in.
And maybe you're the ship.
I'll give you berth wide enough
as befits you, or a small gas giant
which drifts into my purview.
Why, yes, officer, I'll say. That's my wagon.
My newly registered star.

TYPECAST

I used to know the god Apollo.
He taught me acting. I was terrible,
but those old Greeks delight in transformations.
His eyes glittered, sea-like, under Renaissance curls
as he lifted a cigarette to his lips, told me:
All actors should smoke; it's the only way
to do nothing and be completely fascinating.
I hadn't even gotten the hang of beer yet, but I was game.
He liked to have me yell my monologues,
would yell himself, egg me on:
Louder, more, remember how pissed you are!
When I let loose at an imagined jerk of a lover,
Apollo smiled, his teeth little matched pearls
between wine-stained lips. Really, I was a virgin
at everything, from kissing to cards,
but when Apollo is your teacher, you learn some things.
I learned to stand in my tight-fitting, miserable human skin,
and cast it off like a sales-rack coat,
revealing glad rags beneath. And if they were a sham, so what?
I had learned that everything is changeable,
my looks and my loves and my squeamish heart.
That's when Apollo knocked my helmet off.
Careful, he murmured, breath smoky against my ear,
a cook can become a countess, but she'll never burn a cake.
Nothing changes completely. That's where he left me,
with my familiar doubt and newfound sneer,
with the dwindling orange eye
of the cigarette he'd hurled to the stage floor like a dart.

LEANING OUT OF THE AFTERNOONS

I fling my sad nets toward the sea
and haul in old boots strung with bent fishhooks.
The job's a bore.

I fling and I haul, I fling and I haul,
all while half-blinded by glittering waves.
Sounds pretty, I know,

but even the ocean gets old.
Heck, it is old, and a little torn at the seams.
If there be monsters here,

they take the form of gulls
endlessly threading the down-at-heel border
between changeless

and hopeless. They needle the waves
with their laughter.
They suture their throats to the air.

TIME TRAVELER'S HAIBUN: 1989

In the grassy space between the wings of the elementary school and the trailers housing the fifth grade's overflow classrooms, girls flip their hair in imitation of Cindy Crawford, sing *Iko Iko*. None of you know what it means or where the song comes from.

It's honor-roll season, a time of outings to TCBY and Outback Steakhouse. Your mother warns you against filling up on bread, but it's hard to resist the little brown loaves brought warm to the table with soft butter—a luxury that cannot be imagined at home, with its always-refrigerated margarine and Pepperidge Farm sandwich loaves.

Everybody knows what's popular but nobody knows how to act. At ten, you lack any context. The world swims before you, and it constantly stings. Its favorite barb: "Everyone knows that."

Beyond the grassy space of girls is more grass, a quarter-mile loop of track, a church with a painfully white spire, a fence, and a neighborhood maybe a little less nice than yours, crammed between the school and busy Great Neck Road. The fence is of chain link, instead of wooden slats. That's how you know about the niceness—that and the something hard, like a grain of sand, you feel in your mother's voice when she takes you to the school's Spring Fling, where you win another goldfish. They always die, but you're getting better. Now, it takes a while.

Loblollies shiver
in May heat. The world's ending.
The world's a mirage.

NO MYTH

I am a pegasus
and my sister is a pegasus
and we are holding hoof-hands
with yarn-tails safety-pinned to our shorts
as we stand grinning at the Polaroid our mother holds
as our pegasus ears stand pricked on gray hoods
as our yarn-manes descend, fiercely free
to the wings fastened to our wrists with elastic
and I am missing a tooth and my sister has hers and looks
up at the camera with the wonder of a magi approaching a manger
with nothing but a dumb jar of myrrh that nobody has time
to worry about because this is a miracle, that she is a pegasus
with a sister who is a pegasus and a human mother
who owns a Polaroid and feeds her strange daughters Cheerios
and watches fondly as they fly in pink shorts up the stairs.

THE NAVY BRATS

How do you tell a kid, "violence is never the answer,"
when the threat of it puts food on the table,
on his friends' tables, clothes them all
in jeans from J.C. Penney's?

It's more like, "violence isn't always the answer,"
or even, "maybe you shouldn't ask
questions like that," the kind
whose response is squadron-shaped.

Because let's face it: Death's the one
that brought us to the party. And we dance anyway.
It's what we're here for, with our heat-seeking missiles,
our 62-caliber guns.

Still, there's a place and a time. Still, we wait until
we're alone to laugh, to deadpan,
to shake at our seams for the doings
        that will see us come undone.

FAMOUS AMERICAN NAVAL OFFICERS

Keeping tight ships, where no doors stick,
where the stars are not suffered
to twinkle out of regulation.

Who are said to shave
with a blowtorch, and yet
a certain vanity pervades:

never photographed without their caps,
their embroidered scrambled eggs.
And though some—the explorers, mainly—

are rumored to be charming, one
fools not with nitroglycerin,
nor with tar. These men sail hard.

No easy way will do
when bombs fall and rations falter.
When words must form the bulwark

against loneliness and war,
against depths the more inhuman
for how practical they seem.

NO WORD FOR BLUE

having no word for blue,
the ancient greeks invented memory
in place of the sapphires
they craved, the lapis and topazes, lattices
of gleaning they could not name.
the greeks would claim it takes a lot
of goddesses to transport
the slain. it takes alphabets
and scraps of parchment,
takes at least an oral tradition
in which, masked,
with stylized eyebrows,
we recite epics all day and night.
they would say memory is the death blow
to death, the next best thing to blue,
the sky-color,
the sea-color,
the stone-color,
the color of eternity,
the color of shell beads,
the color I remember
of my rivals' eyes,
of my dress in the temple,
of the mirage of your earrings,
of the teeth of our laughter,
of the night we once met in,
of the ink in the diaries

of men
who never returned.

THE GOOD SHIP *GOOD NIGHT*

My neighbor has outfitted the light
to the left of his door with a red bulb,
and the light to the right with a green,
as if his home were a ship, as if
it could drift in the night, as if
it could hit another home unmoored
in gloom, its poor unwary passengers
all wrecked and broken but for some pilot
who knows the roads and markers,
who gently steers the home about the shoals
abutting the gutters, makes fast
as dawn comes alongside daffodils
and ash trees, anchoring the home
with oaks, with the reality
that daylight people agree on—
the one where houses are solid, safe,
unmoving, heedless of the tides.

A TEN-HOUR VIDEO OF A TRAIN GOING THROUGH NORWAY

We chat; I interrupt
to let you know

a tunnel's coming up.
A house. That the river

we saw on the right
is now on the left.

Must have happened
when we went over

that bridge too high
to see down from.

Mountains stay
vastly plastered

to the horizon
like blue gumdrops.

The train makes
an elephant noise

each time it passes
a certain sign. We think

at first it means
a road's coming up,

but sometimes there's
no road. Just the sign,

seeming to say: O Train,
be in high spirits.

And the train responds to that.

I LOVE YOUR TEETH

Remember that time I caught a heel
in hotel shag and fell down a flight of stairs?
Out of the dazzling dark I rose into light after light,
the gleam off your teeth—a whole band's worth
of sheet music, thirty-two freight trains hurtling into town,
pocketful of fun-time pills, heavy flour sacks
to hoodwink famine, sailors on parade, Victorian
specimen drawer of catalogued trilobites, shelf
of new notebooks in September, taut laundered sheets
awaiting tourist season, blank checks I could sign my name to,
the pearly picket that guards the yard from which you called me home.

ECHOCARDIOGRAM

The doctors have a question for my heart.
They send it by singing messenger,

a baton that probes my ribs with sound.
On a nearby screen, it forms the image

of a four-mouthed fist. Its flutter traces
a beat like this:

> *connect / correct / correct / connect*

Later, the doctors will decide what it means,
how long it can go on. They'll deliver results

in their usual way: by unassuming envelope.
I'll rip it open to the tune I've started imagining

an end to. I think, maybe there'll be no fade-out.
Quick silence. Burst of hurried, uncertain applause.

RESPONSIBILITY

Because there are no beds in Observation,
I spend the night in Pediatrics,
where the nurses and I are glad together
there are no children.
Every little one of them is well
tonight in the state of Maine,
not staring, as I am,
at the pain chart marked with frowny faces,
not cobwebbed with ledes,
tethered to machines that mark
every breath and pulse.
When the nurses look in at 3 a.m.,
I take my doses meekly.
And when they let me go tomorrow afternoon,
I'll have called the new prescriptions in.
I'll have neatly squared the edges
of the anti-bullying brochures,
as if responsibility could dissolve
the hard, white shapes on the scan.

THE LOST

And I was afraid, loving
what I knew would be lost.
—Wendell Berry

Every day, a species, a lake, a language—
with so much poised to slip away,
I figured it safest to fix my affections
on what had already disappeared.
That's how I became an ardent expert on the lost,
lavishing long hours
on colonies, princes, pilots, civilizations
irretrievable, secure.
Deep in obsession's narrow focus, drawing
hearts around the photo of the drowned starlet,
I could hardly hear

you, shuffling through the house
like an unquiet spirit,
alive and losable and wondering
exactly where it was I'd gone.

WHERE THEIR HEARTS WERE KEPT

That woman's heart was in horses,
and this one's in the bayou.
Their friend, a raucous blond,
split hers between California and corgis.
Another gave hers to birdsong
in the pine boughs.
This one to the smokestacks of a factory
on the edge of the plains,
and that one to the cedar water tower
guarding a rooftop in the Bronx.
They knew an older woman with gunmetal curls
who kept hers in a casserole dish,
its blue enamel chipped. For years,
her grandmother had used that dish
for seven-layer dip. These women knew
other women whose hearts were trapped
in beat-up cars beside abandoned barns,
inside the suitcases their fathers took when they left,
tucked into plastic daisies in veterans' cemeteries
in Iowa, in France. Still others wore
their hearts pinned to their chests,
pumping where everyone could see.
Some women thought those women brave,
and others foolish. But terrifying?
Yes, on that everyone agreed.

SYCORAX AND CO.

So strong she could control the moon.
   But dead before our story starts.
If there's weakness in us, a tragic flaw,

   it's no different for witches.
They can enchant anyone but themselves.
   So strong she could control the moon,

bear children, imprison her enemies in pine trees,
   she wasn't strong enough not to die.
If that weakness in her, that tragic flaw,

   left her where you and I will someday be—
gone—what use was there in growing
   so strong she could control the moon?

She's offstage now, while we carry on.
   Or we could try it this way. Say what feels
like weakness to us, a tragic flaw,

   was satisfaction. Having done all she wished,
she was done with all. If we become
   so strong we could control the moon,
but see weakness there—our magic's flawed.

C STUDENT

To learn to be present in the moment,
I follow the example
of the daffodil
seen from the window,
yawning in slow motion,
the toucan-colored sideways saucer
and its cup. But—
what's the lesson again?
Something to do, I think, with rain.
Or maybe it's forbearance.
Pestilence? A plot point
from a Victorian novel?
The daffodil nods its chin
like a teacher, prompting,
but it's no use.
In the face of reality,
reality's the thing I forget.

JANUARY

We're in for snow, not penance.
The dark evening clings like sap
to wild maple-branch lace.

No Puritan, this new year.

A young man on ample haunches,
he sashays past the backyard's arborvitae
lined up like a soldiers' picket,
hoping to share a smoke.

In the house, more than one radio on,
tuned to different stations. A sound
like Mission Control out of reach. Oh yes

      "the marvelous is available to everyone,"
says David Gascoyne from the brittle pages
of a 1982 reprint of *A Short Survey of Surrealism*.

Rubbing our ankles with the soles of our feet,
making the sighs and hmms of being alive
as if it were worth talking about
                  (it's all we talk about!)

And last year's flowerpots drift in the snowpack

burnt sugar dusk persistent non-roar
of the highway over the river
that uses the thick light like pomade

THE WORLD'S MOST BEAUTIFUL WISTERIA TREE

My family posts photos of fish that they've caught.
My family posts photos of trucks on the ice.
The internet bursts with measurements.
27 inches of fish.
3 tons of truck.
1 and ½ feet of ice.
1 ton of family.
5 megabytes of photos.
1 millisecond to click "like."
1 millisecond times 10 times 10,000.
The internet bursts with approval.
Smiley face with teeth. Smiley face with tongue.
I heart it. I wow it.
New York's most instagrammable subway station distracts me
for 2 minutes exact.
A purse shaped like a dinosaur.
The world's most beautiful wisteria tree.
A meme about Persephone.
Another big fish.
A great northern pike, now. A muskie.
At my desk beside a window-wide view of chickadees and snow,
I watch the internet burst from the weight of its fish.
I like it.
I heart it.
The family falling out of the internet
as I follow. I filter. I scroll.

NEUTRAL STATE

The no-green season.
Sorry flurries wrinkle down
from a sky the ivory-gray of parchment paper
after cod's been cooked on it,
half-translucent, partly oiled.

The spicebush we bought at last year's Audubon sale
and never planted
is trying to weather out the season in the garage,
its leaves a curling curry-yellow.

In downtown Portland, a blinking chyron:
Call Joe
        Call Joe
on the Time and Temperature Building.

SUNSTRUCK

In shade,
this place resembles
the world's most boring photograph:

dim whites, muddy browns,
washed-out grays
like someone
stuck tape over them,
not a deep velvet
Ansel Adams abyss.

But a little early sunlight
filtered through birches
turns everything glam,
the river's ice now sea green and turquoise
as if Florida were surging up,
a dizzy bird dazed by the daily swing
of magnetic north,
looping the arctic circle
in fifty-mile chunks.

My shadow's the color of a rock star's eyelids,
a shade called lagoon
or blue heaven, sunpony,
devilrider.

This is why polar explorers go mad:

not the cold
but the contrast.

THE OWLS

We've had so much thaw followed by so much freeze
that the remaining snow is thick-slicked in ice,
and the owls are starving,
unable to penetrate the stiff crust for mice.
Out of the woods they come
to stalk our suet-feeders,
take out squirrels, bluebirds, other owls.
When they glide up from the maples in silent flight,
their long wingtips seem like luck's own arrows.
Their luck is wearing thin, but ours is good.
We've always wanted to see them,
and can't help our wonder when we do,
becoming as joyful and suddenly fearless
as field mice
in their hard-roofed, subnivean hells.

TRENDSETTER

Prolonged bronze of new spring leaves.
Why don't they come up green?

Are they afraid of the change of seasons?
Like, Old Man Winter will come after them
if they're too sassy?

Hermit thrush in the bare branches,
same color as the bare branches, last year's leaves.

Camouflage is the new black.
The only unfashionable one here is the sky,
blue as a dream.

Maybe it'll start a trend.
Maybe the sky doesn't have any predators.
Maybe that pampered atmosphere
lives in luxury—

    thinks about something
   other than what might eat it,
   what it has to eat.

AFTER BASHO

a golden shovel

I called my dear ones from
the lakes and villages, said I'd had all
the square meals I could stand, would replace these
casseroles and puddings with the sight of trees.
But they couldn't take the idea in—
they brought me salads
they brought me soups—
they piled dishes everywhere, everywhere,
when I had eyes only for the cherry
branch outside my window. I watched its blossoms,
like tiny tortillas, flex and fill and fall.

YELLOW BIRDS

A long-form luxury,
the Peterson's guide.
You can leisurely examine
the golden slippers
of the snowy egret,
the lemon-peel eyes
of a sharp-shinned hawk.
You can wallow in the primrose
chevron of a cedar waxwing's tail,
a mustardy mallard beak.
Outside, it's different.
Knowing some streaky thing
at a thin glance
      "with your help, we might do it"
as the greater yellowlegs
the lesser yellowlegs
killdeer, woodcock
or a flash-in-the-pan
Canada warbler
      "the first one we've seen this year"
"you'll get a stiff neck like that"
is a tough call
to make
      "something for the life list"
never used to nest here
but there's a lot of them now

EARLY MORNING, JUNE

Fledgling starlings' ugly vocals
wind right up my spine.
I shouldn't say it, but wouldn't mind
if the new-to-the-neighborhood
bobtail cat
with eyes like a lynx
whittled down their number.

He's good for it.
The other day I saw him
prance out from behind the shed
like a royal prince,
something limp in his mouth.

Bleach-white sunlight attacks the pines.
Two doors down, Mr. Edward
            pulls the cover
from his classic Cougar.
Engine rev caresses air,
gives my ears a rinse.

AN INTRODUCTION

Hello. I am a bog.

There are turtles in me.
And frogspawn.

Blackbirds yell in my willow trees.
A muskrat likes to ruffle

my surfaces.
They reflect clouds:
white, gray, and white again.

They reflect hawks high and shining.
There are sometimes lilies in my hair,
sometimes dry leaves.

When I sing, I use a minnow voice,
fleet and tiny, prone to harmonies.

I will be happy
to continue
with you
in a moment
but now
please excuse me:

a heron is stalking my belly
with its dinosaur eye

while the wind
makes
a flute

of my back.

SHAMELESS

The zinnias sweat.

They drip color
that stops
the garden

like a shout,
trips the tomatoes
in their cages,

gets the sunflowers
shaking their heads.
The zinnias drool

scarlet and lime,
they strain at their stalks,
froth their loud fists

in the face of the sun.
They stir wantonness
and I want it.

I want whatever they'll share.

A BEGGAR'S RIDE

Emerging from October mists,
the wild turkeys and I meet.
I stand decorously still.

The turkeys decide—slowly,
carefully—to proceed.
Then they startle

                as I shift
my impatient weight.
                They swerve

as if, on my two blunt feet
in the fog, square-toothed
and fat with choices, I were a monster.

I have something to say to that.
And that something is *yes*.

Turkeys, let it be true.

This world is chockablock
with death and joy and hazard,
and it would be right for a woman alone
to be its scariest thing.

A PERSONALITY TEST

In the orchard, I catch
out of the corner
of my eye
a black rag
snapped tight
in the wind.

Turns out to be
a field mouse
racing
across fallen leaves,
tumbling
in and out of pocks

like a Marine recruit,
all *go!go!go!*
purely exposed
to the eyes of hawks,
foxes, whatever
wants to eat her,

which is everything.
As I watch,
she disappears
into divots, reappears,
slides, carroms, and slaloms,
a little dark clown.

I can't help it—
I laugh at her pratfalls.
I laugh at her fear.
I laugh at her fear.
I laugh
as she runs
for her life.

DAMMED

Trying to rise
from the unleafed thicket
of my body, I only get so far.

It's okay, I tell myself,
to feel slow and lightless.
Take your cue
from the sap dammed
in this mapled acreage.
It's not going anywhere

because it isn't time.
The sun hasn't surprised
bare branches
with a sense of looseness yet, started
the thaw-and-freeze beat
that clears spring's throat.

Meanwhile, the snow-glazed trees
only look like microphones
switched to off,
waiting backstage
in the dark for some juice.

They've got the juice already.
It's just that they love the suspense.

Think of that,
I think, flexing

my ankles and wrists
in tiny circles
beneath my leaden comforter.
Think of how the sugar
builds beneath the bark

in gulping, golden gallonfuls.

Think of yourself like that,
a river rising under the ice,
soon to crank into spillover.
Think how your gorgeousness
will burst singing from the tap.

SHOUT YES

I am the god of lilacs.
God of thin winter branches, bare.
The white-to-purple clusters that overbear
your Junes, swell summer into scented overload,
they find their headwaters here: in snow.
In ground dazzle-dusted with frost.
Come to my temple. I'll teach you
hardship's the offering I like best.
I'll teach you to tip tight buds
into subzero winds, tilt your teeth
toward unearthly blooms,
shout yes, I'll live through this.

AT THE POINT

This landscape's style
is white t-shirt
over black jeans
faded grey.

It's an affectation, yes,
but not the one you're thinking of.

The holes in the snowpack
not pre-distressed in-factory.
The cotton-colored hills
genuinely freaking out
along the river's icy denim.

There's this noise
like a flame trying to catch.
That snow pocked as a moonscape.
Those trees like boiled silverware.

Something has grown too heavy.
The land hushes like an angry father.

That's how you know
it's time to leave
or get small,
unnoticeable,
another birch tree
peeling

because
something's about to break.

MY UN-NERUDAN DESPAIR

No shipwrecks, no ocean,
no flowering in the mud.

I'm not sure despair should feel so unoperatic.
Like a waiting room stocked
with four-year-old issues of GQ.

Just now, idly reaching out, I snuffed the life
from a gnat that's haunted my office
for days, casually snapping

my fingers closed, flexing them open to find
the black stain of its body
pasted to my palm.

I don't remember
"the hour of the spell that blazed like a lighthouse."
And whether "there is fire in your tombs,"
I don't recall.

Instead, I dully dispense
death to the winged.

I grow mossy
in disinterested detention,
mortaring the days over myself like a wall.

WHEN I AM EMPTY, PLEASE DISPOSE OF ME PROPERLY

Attending the notes of my own fallibility,
I sit in the Performance Studies library,
fat headphones like cinnamon buns clamped to my ears.

I hear Puck, waiting his turn in the rafters.
Billie Holiday's wry, regretful voice—

> *These foolish things . . .*

This world is lousy with questions.
What is the most popular sunshine in your state?
Which mask is better: Nixon, butterfly, clown?

In the old days, when the gods were kind, they'd just give you
    the answer.
How to choose, how to live.
They'd come down on a cloud like an elevator.

> *. . . remind me of you*

Dust motes float in library air,
gorgeous spangles formed from skin and dead stars.
The sun hammers its performative gold into the
    floorboards,

reminds me of the choices
I make with every ticking second,
my motivations modernist, unclear.

MASTERFUL

All the voices speak.
At once but not together.

All the voices have something to say.
Demands mostly.

And scolding.
All the voices want me to know

who's boss. That I'm not.
That I'm little, corroded,

a scab with a face that frowns
and why couldn't I try

harder, do more, be masterful?
Why couldn't I act

like all the voices,
the voices suddenly silenced

as my dim-bulb brain's distracted
by a huge moon and the thought:

What if basketballs had skeletons?
Wouldn't they look

just like that? O, all the voices,
I'm not so sure I'm sorry

to be so useless,
in love with useless things.

SUGGESTED ADMISSION: $20

In the Museum of Apologies, there is a whole wing for the half-assed.

A small display of the abject is surrounded by equally modest collections of the sincere, heartfelt, and profound.

The museum's board, drunk on conference presentations about community engagement, demands exhibits that juice ticket sales.

> A gala devoted to *Dear John* letters, with their pre-emptive *it's-not-yous*.

> The atrium's somber Victorian velvets replaced by a celebration of sorry not sorry texts, memes, and social media posts.

> A three-day series of panels on whether corporate communications should eschew apologies for expressions of gratitude for the recipients' patience.

We are all patients in the sickroom that is the Museum of Apologies.

We suffer the comorbidities of regret and expectation.

You will be expected, as you leave the museum, to return the bright, aluminum button clipped to your collar. We regret any inconvenience.

We regret everything, officially.

But if there's anything we're sorry for at heart, sorry like a moan, it's that we're not you—

    stepping out into impudent daylight, free of the pretense of shame.

THE WORST THAT COULD HAPPEN

You're lost. The gunmen don't speak English. You forgot you had a test and you're naked and it's a shop test and you crush something vital in the drill press. You make a scene at a dinner party. You drop a dime off the Washington Monument and it kills the First Lady. You drop a dime on the President and wind up in a windowless room in Langley. Your ears fall off. Your toes turn green. Your stomach rejects cheese. You're a city of tiny monsters, waiting to be fed. You get mustard on your guayabera and your drycleaner won't even look at you. Your gray hairs start a Facebook group. Your best friend is perfect and you kill her in a fit of rage. It's not worthy of Shakespeare. It's petty. Your sleeves are too short. A beggar startles you from your superhero reverie and you're too cross to part with a quarter. You cheat on your taxes. You vote Republican without even believing in it. You drink to forget. You forget to drink and die of dehydration. Your teeth are crooked. Your kids are dirty hippies. The dog growls at you. At night, the wolves come. It's raining. No one likes you. You're alone. Your teeth are still crooked. Your only friend is a cactus. You're afraid. You're afraid. You love your wife and eat well and greet the sunshiny morning with vigor and you're afraid.

WE ARE ALL TERRIBLE

You are married to my ex-boyfriend.
And you, and you, and you.
I mean, I don't know you
but I knew my ex-boyfriends
and I know they've married,
so I know that you and you and you exist.
It's been long enough
that I hope they're happy.
I hope you're happy.
I hope they grew out of the reasons
they became ex-boyfriends.
I haven't grown out of anything at all,
but oh!—you there, narrowing your eyes
as if I were a skunk or a setting sun,
it's true! I married your ex-boyfriend!
We're very much in love
and just as annoying together
as we were individually.
With our horse laughs
and emotional avoidance,
and now, our couples' yoga class.
It's funny, really, isn't it?—
How well
everything's worked out.

AND ALWAYS LAUGHS AT YOUR STUPID JOKES

Love forgot your name on the way to Walmart,
came back with seeds for the bird feeder just the same.
Always been hazy on personal details, Love, but good
at the trivialities of care. Whether your hair is black
or blond, Love can't seem to recall, but knows you
should be easier on yourself. Love flings a hand
across you reflexively while braking, always reminds you
of your doctor's appointments, once biked over
the bridge to bring you a flower, has a habit of staring
deep into your eyes with eyes just a bit unfocused.
As if relaxing into your image. As if you could be anyone.
You could be anyone, Love thinks, and still I would be there.

TOMORROW, I'LL TELL PEOPLE IT WAS FOOD POISONING

Feeling vaguely fin de siècle, languorously ill,
                as if consumption, as if wasting

     but just wasted

            tho' a little pink wine ne'er should hurt me—
avoiding
          bright light since morning and
               one eye open like an overcooked egg:

               the whites rubbery, the irises chalked
               like a hopscotch with fake sunshiny cheer.

How does this happen at 37?
     Rippling the bathwater, unrequited by images
          of alternate paths with babies and studios but
          I am beached here—

The path to heaven is paved with cockleshells.
     Mineral wings absent of meat.

I am not tired yet of anything but not knowing how to live.

THE SIDES

On the path through the meadow, a pile
of what looks like an old explosion
of milkweed seeds. Up close, I find
it's feathers—downy, curly, gray.
Feathers and a bloody, yellow foot.
This prey, probably a junco. The predator,
probably a hawk. Here's where I think
the camera should pull back
into the clouds, the meadow
getting smaller as I'm hurried up
into the heavens by an angel
for a luminous appointment
that will explain this small death
or at least let me know whose side
to be on. Watching the cold world disappear,
dizzy from speed and lack of air,
I grasp at the angel's wings,
come away with a fistful of down.

BEAUTIFUL NOW

Aging, he grew sure the country was gone to hell
not because of me, but people too much like me
for me to tell the difference. And yet
he'd shown me how to mound dark soil,
firm and careful, around a cucumber seedling
to help it grow. Had let me drive the tractor
or pretend, sitting on his lap as he puffed
his pipe and smiled into the sky. Let me braid
the strands of his combover and clamp
the ends with pink barrettes. Back then,
when I lifted a mirror to his face,
he'd turned one cheek and then the other.
I'm beautiful now, he said,
        and he was.

SHARE THE WEALTH

Even the dying waste time. They too admire
the lavish ways of the spendthrift—lighting cigars
with c-notes, too lazy to gather the diamonds
they let fall and sure, why not, a round on me
and let's dance? Skinflints slinging dimes
at the poor don't rate our sympathy; their slender charity—
a pale hand thrusting through a cracked door—
is nothing to them, or to us.

             If we must die, let's do it richly,
in a froth of hours lost to solitaire, reading
a favorite book for the fiftieth time, naps, baking, staring
into space—space so hangdog in its vastness,
what miser wouldn't rush to fill it? Not us. We'll pour back
all the wealth we've got into the dream from which we came.

THEY CAN'T ALL BE POLAR BEARS

Among pecan leaves and sweet gum,
here comes a caterpillar as long as a hot dog.
Do not kill it, the naturalists urge.
If biodiversity means otters, giraffes,
and sloths, it also means 6-inch, green,
multi-segmented walking tubes
of toothpaste with barbed antlers protruding
at regular intervals from their backs.
It means the Hickory Horned Devil, larvae
of the rust-red, fuzzy, Regal Moth,
flapping its egg-laden way toward a pecan
through the alarming southern night.

WHAT DID THE HOLY BOOK GET WRONG?

Wear whatever cloth you want.

You still can't eat shrimp,
but that's because they have nice personalities.

I give you permission
not to honor your father and mother
if
they are complete psychos, but don't
write them off too quick—

a lot of stuff that seems bad now
will look, if not better, then more pitiable over time.

That's my problem.
Too much perspective.

Given eons, my dilemmas solve themselves.

Love's still kind, but I should have defined "kindness."
It means treating people better than they deserve.

If you'd like to emulate me,
I don't recommend it.

But if you won't have it any other way,
be slow to anger, a time bomb
only someone hellbent can hook up.

Don't treat just any of the ignorant
to your incandescent flame.

UNACCENTED

God's first language is silence.
His second, heat.
He learned mercy next,
though he still has trouble with the pronunciations.
Then Aramaic, Igbo, Old High German.
God is a completist,
proud to understand every earthly prayer.
But if you've studied languages, you know
comprehension's the easy part.
Much harder to say something back
without using
your mother tongue.

LET'S WELCOME OUR NEXT CONTESTANT

Every so often, America
rediscovers its beating heart
through the medium of the game show.

Those that survive, on TV
and in our memories, better attest
to our nature than any monument.

Consider: This commonwealth
of eggheads has watched
Jeopardy! for 45 years.

Wheel of Fortune requires
both outward pleasantness
and inward cunning, while

The Price Is Right and *Let's Make
a Deal* marry a huckster's
cash-crop spirit with

a willingness to play the fool—
so long as it pays. Land
of the brave, of the penny-wise

and pound-foolish, I've seen
thunderheads slam your parched prairies,
your cities drown in swamp water.

I've watched fogs thicker
than your own coarse-carded cotton
muffle your brain, and still

you buzz in, frenetic
as a coke-addled hornet.
You're the nation that thinks

vowels can be bought, an answer
can take the form of a question,
that only quitters quit at a dinette set.

There's something a little—
okay, a lot—wrong with you,
wrong with us, but of all

our national diseases,
the refusal to lose
might be the only one

I wouldn't care to cure—
the way that when the survey says *chance*,
what we hear is *guarantee*.

IT'S WHEATGRASS FROM HERE ON OUT

O twentysomethings of Sunday at 10 a.m., unsteady
on your pins, pie-eyed and looking for the hair of the dog,
I too have been sloshed, hammered, tanked, blitzed.
One over the eight and three sheets to the wind, I've wound
my nightly way, jober as a sudge, from bed to toilet and back.
I've rousted my pot-valiant, rat-legged ass out into mornings
only mimosas could love, sunglassed and shuddering.
Over omelets, I've met my fellow slozzled tosspots
for a salutary swig, winced with them through the pains
of the sauced. Now I'm twenty years older, one table over,
and if it looks like I'm sniffing at you over the rim
of my prim smoothie (shot of wheatgrass, baby spinach,
positively brimming with antioxidants), I'm not. Just surprised—
its own kind of inebriation—at how young you seem, at myself
for assuming I'd do things differently, if I could do them over again.

THE BOYS OF SUMMER

If you liked my favorite song,
you'd treat me just the same
as you do now, hating it,
and that's how I know you love me.

Like you love planets and Ralph Waldo Emerson—
for themselves and despite themselves,
because they're surprising.

I don't think that way about myself,
but I'm not the one that loves me.
I'm the one that loves you

and that's what surprises you, I guess.
Like when you look up from your desk and there's a sunset
that turns, at the last second, very slightly purple.

Like you somehow should have known it but still—
it's the most wonderful news.

CATCH YOUR BREATH

> Once I tasted time I never wanted anything else.
>
> – Eileen Myles

During the high season of yellow flowers,
whip hawkweed, tansy, St John's wort and goldenrod,
I was stuck in bed, relearning how to breathe.
I heard all the inefficient exchanges.
You downstairs, the click of a pop-tab,
the little hiss of air straight from a commercial.
The promise of heat in the morning's stillness.
A symptom, I've learned, of what nearly killed me
is a feeling of dread. As if I could use that information.
As if now, when I can walk again in the orchard
without spiraling my heart rate up, my oxygen down,
the flowers weren't faded and wrung out. On the pond,
a last lily pad tipped on its side like a showboat's paddlewheel.
Things sink and merge. They become. The windblown trees,
fallen pears, my footprints, the memorial stone
whose carvings lichen has rendered illegible.
I'm walking here, or my shadow is. I'm walking,
or a memory is. A breath condensed in air.

THE GREEN GRASS

I would rather be
the mottled frog
in the leaf litter
than the chihuahua
in the little hat.

I would rather be
the chihuahua
with all its shivers
than the woman
juggling conference calls.

I would rather be
the woman sighing
with frustration
than the man whose child
has blocked his number.

I would rather be
that child than the one
who never came home.
Bliss is relative,
the frog says,

thinking of pots
of salted water warming
as he shudders,
overlooked
and alive in the leaves.

NOTES

This book's first epigraph is inscribed (with the delineation reproduced here) on the wall of a casino in Macau. The second appears in *Japanese Death Poems* (Hoffman, ed., Charles E. Tuttle Publishing Co., Inc. 1986).

"MPH" is a loose response/engagement with James Schuyler's poem "Freely Espousing," in Schuyler's *Collected Poems* (FSG, 1993).

The title and first line of "Leaning out of the Afternoon" are a play on the title and first line of Pablo Neruda's "Inclinado en las tardes," while "My Un-Nerudan Despair" is a response to Neruda's "La canción desesperada," with quotations from W.S. Merwin's English translation: Pablo Neruda, *Twenty Love Poems and a Song of Despair* (W.S. Merwin, trans., Penguin Books, 2004).

The epigraph to "The Lost" is taken from Wendell Berry's poem "Song in a Year of Catastrophe," in *The Selected Poems of Wendell Berry* (Counterpoint, 1998).

"After Basho": The golden shovel is a poetic form invented by Terrance Hayes, and first used in his poem "The Golden Shovel." In the form, each sequential line of a poem ends with a word that, if read in order, recreates another, earlier poem. The original poem that inspired (and can be read in) "After Basho" is a haiku by Matsuo Basho, as translated into English by Robert Hass.

The phrase "with your help, we might do it" in "Yellow Birds" is spoken by Les McCann as he introduces the song "Cold Duck Time" (written by Eddie Harris) on the album *Swiss Movement*.

"What Did the Holy Book Get Wrong?" is based on a prompt from Kyle Dargan, and a question posed by Zanne Langlois.

The first line of "Unaccented" is a saying attributed to Saint John of the Cross.

"The Boys of Summer" is a wonderful song and we should all be grateful to Don Henley and Mike Campbell for it.

The epigraph to "Catch Your Breath" is taken from Eileen Myles' book-length essay *For Now* (Yale University Press, 2020).

ACKNOWLEDGMENTS

Poems from this book have appeared in a number of journals, sometimes under different titles and in slightly different forms:

Cartagena Journal: "Famous American Naval Officers"

Cherry Tree: "Typecast"

Columbia Poetry Review: "And Always Laughs at Your Stupid Jokes," "C Student," "They Can't All Be Polar Bears," "It's Wheatgrass from Here on Out," and "Let's Welcome Our Next Contestant"

The Fourth River: "Dammed" (as "February, Maine") and "The Sides"

The Kenyon Review Online: "Tomorrow, I'll Tell People It Was Food Poisoning," "Leaning Out of the Afternoons," and "We Are All Terrible"

Little Dog Poetry: "The Good Ship 'Good Night'"

On the Seawall: "I Love Your Teeth"

Pine Hills Review: "A Personality Test," "My Un-Nerudan Despair," and "Share the Wealth" (as "Fiesta")

phoebe: "The Worst that Could Happen"

Ploughshares: "Beautiful Now"

PoetryNow (Podcast): "Time Traveler's Haibun: 1989"

Sixth Finch: "At the Point" and "Where Their Hearts Were Kept"

Stonecoast Review: "No Word for Blue"

the tiny: "The World's Most Beautiful Wisteria Tree"

Typo: "Sunstruck"

All my thanks to Zanne Langlois, Amy Bergen, and Meg Stout, in whose company I wrote the first drafts of many of these poems. Thanks also to the teachers and workshop leaders without whose prompts and readings many of these poems would not exist, most particularly Hoa Nguyen and Celeste Doaks. Thanks to Sandra Beasley and Kathleen Ossip for advice regarding line edits and organization. My thanks as well to the amazing members of Kathleen's manuscript organization workshop: Carlo André, Emily Blair, Marietta Brill, Susan Goodman, BC Griffith, Liz Johnson, Leah Kaminski, Jen Levitt, John Del Peschio, and Yuki Tanaka.

Deep thanks to Joanna Fuhrman, Jennifer L. Knox, and Kathleen Ossip for their generous blurbs.

My gratitude to Veliz Books and its publisher, Lau Cesarco Eglin, for believing in this book and seeing it into the light of day.

And last but never least, thanks to Jeff Eaton, the king of Jeffs, "with Jeff knows what and Jeff knows why."